MINDFULNESS

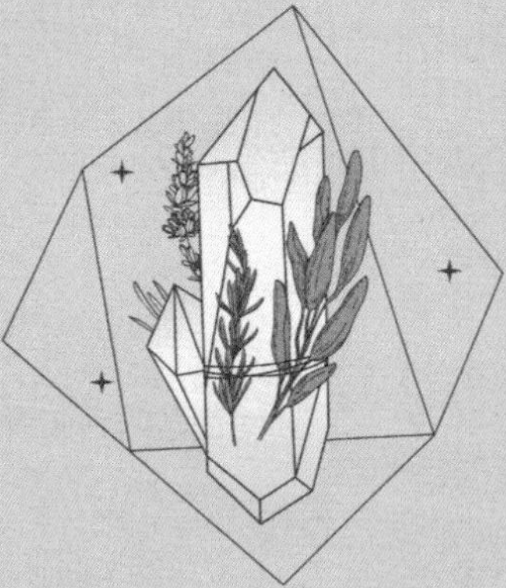

MINDFULNESS

Meditations & Inspirations

MANDALA
San Rafael · Los Angeles · London

Be HAPPY
in the
moment.
That's
ENOUGH.

—MOTHER TERESA

Let go
of your mind,
and then be
MINDFUL.
Close your eyes
and LISTEN!

—RUMI

The soul aids the body and, at certain moments, raises it. It is the only bird which bears up its own cage.

—VICTOR HUGO

I knew life
Began where
I stood in
the DARK,
Looking out
into the
LIGHT.

—YUSEF KOMUNYAKAA

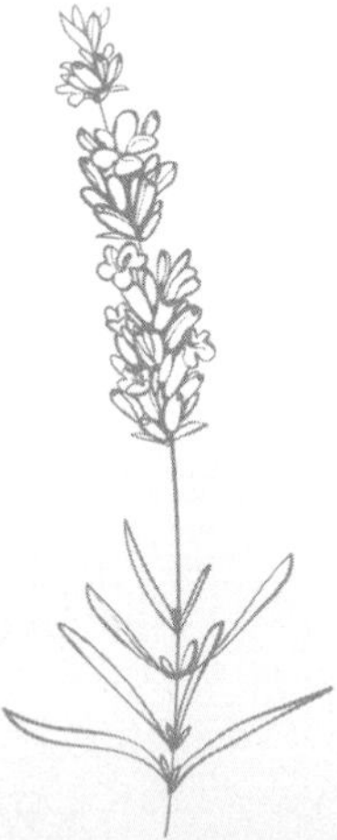

PARADISE ON EARTH IS WHERE I AM.

—Voltaire

A MIND SET IN ITS WAYS IS WASTED.

—Eric Schmidt

The mind is
never right
but when it is
AT PEACE
within itself.

—SENECA

I am
HAPPY
and
CONTENT
because I
think I am.

—ALAIN-RENÉ LESAGE

HAPPINESS
is where we
find it, but very
rarely where we
seek it.

—J. Petit-Senn

PEOPLE DON'T GET UPSET. THEY CONTRIBUTE TO THEIR UPSETNESS.

—Albert Ellis

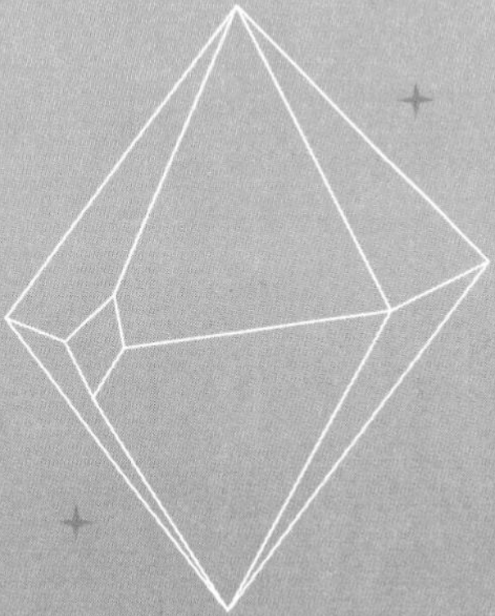

Focus more
on your
DESIRE than
on your
DOUBT, and
the dream
will take care
of itself.

—MARK TWAIN

Your MIND
will answer
most questions
if you learn
to RELAX
and wait for
the answer.

—WILLIAM S. BURROUGHS

AS SOON AS
YOU TRUST
YOURSELF,

YOU WILL KNOW HOW TO LIVE.

—Johann Wolfgang von Goethe

Anyone who
reads a book
with a sense
of obligation
does not
understand
the ART
of reading.

—LIN YUTANG

A SIMPLE
life is
its own
REWARD.

—GEORGE SANTAYANA

The
UNEXAMINED
life is
NOT WORTH
living.

—SOCRATES

Do not
wait until the
conditions are
perfect to begin.
Beginning makes
the conditions
PERFECT.

—ALAN COHEN

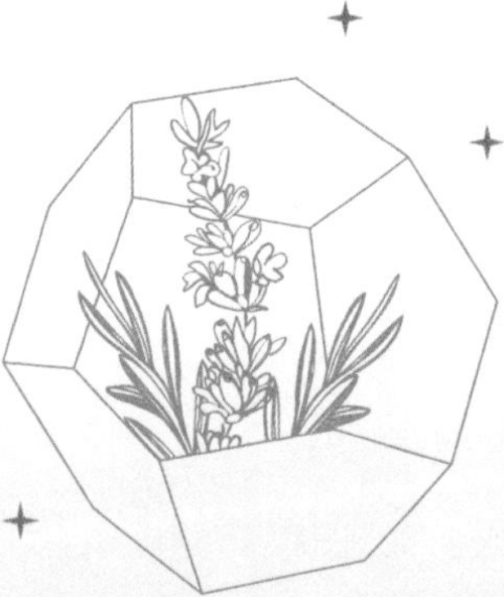

We can
never obtain
peace in
the outer world
until we make
peace with
ourselves.

—DALAI LAMA XIV

To have
the feeling,
to-day or
any day I am
SUFFICIENT
as I am!

—Walt Whitman

Mindfulness is
not a mechanical
process. It is
developing a

very gentle, kind,
and creative
awareness to the
present moment.

—AMIT RAY

IT DOES
NOT MATTER
HOW SLOWLY
YOU GO,
AS LONG
AS YOU DO
NOT STOP.

—Confucius

The stiller
you are, the
calmer life is.

—RASHEED OGUNLARU

Whatever diverts the mind from itself may help.

—BERNARD MALAMUD

Sometimes when
FORTUNE
scowls most
spitefully, she
is preparing
her most
dazzling gifts.

—WINSTON CHURCHILL

Look past your thoughts so you may drink the pure nectar of THIS MOMENT.

—RUMI

Nothing
can bring you
peace but
YOURSELF.

—RALPH WALDO
EMERSON

Life isn't
about waiting
for the storm
to pass but
learning to
DANCE IN
THE RAIN.

—VIVIAN GREENE

The ability to
OBSERVE
without
EVALUATING
is the highest
form of
INTELLIGENCE.

—JIDDU KRISHNAMURTI

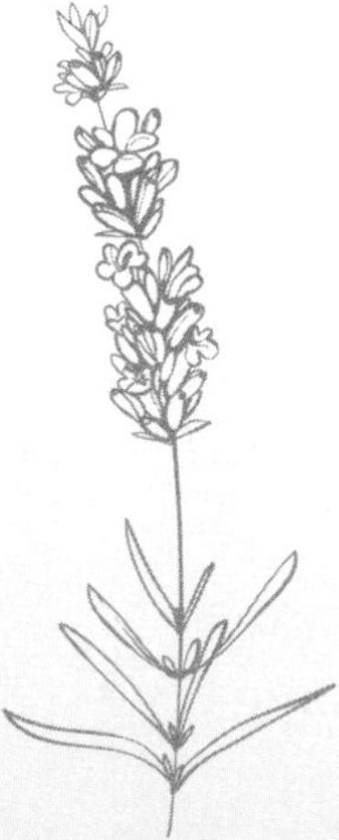

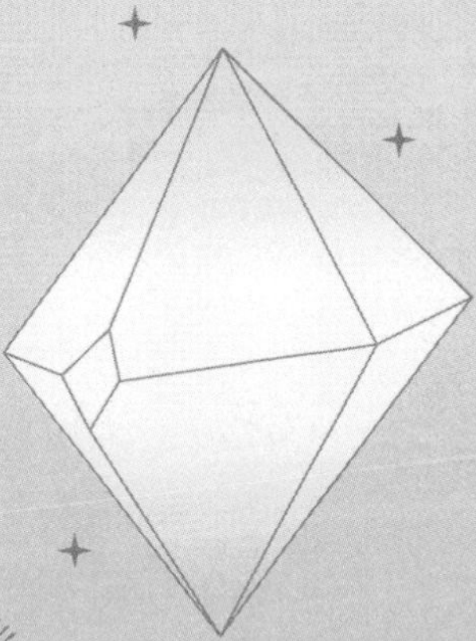

Much of spiritual life is self-acceptance, maybe all of it.

—JACK KORNFIELD

FEELINGS
COME AND
GO LIKE
CLOUDS IN A
WINDY SKY.

CONSCIOUS BREATHING IS MY ANCHOR.

—Thích Nhất Hạnh

Change your
THOUGHTS,
and you
change your
WORLD.

—NORMAN VINCENT PEALE

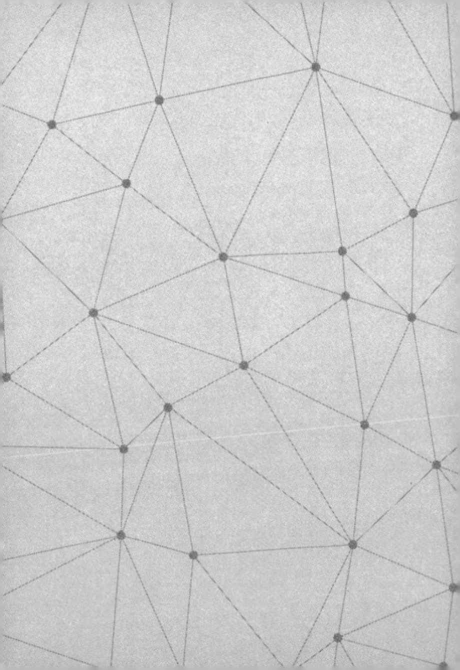

We can
complain because
rose bushes
have thorns or
rejoice because
thorn bushes
have roses.

—ABRAHAM LINCOLN

Distraction wastes our energy; concentration restores it.

—SHARON SALZBERG

TO THINE
OWN SELF
BE TRUE.

—William Shakespeare

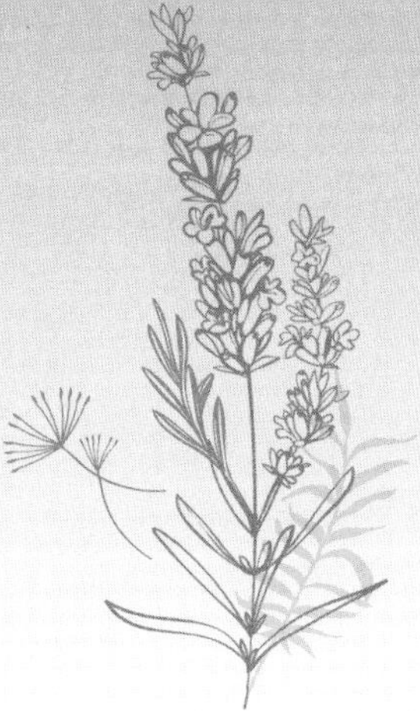

The true secret
of happiness
lies in taking a
genuine interest
in all the details
of daily life.

—WILLIAM MORRIS

Mindfulness means being AWAKE. It means really knowing what you are doing.

—JON KABAT-ZINN

WE ARE
WHAT WE
REPEATEDLY
DO.

EXCELLENCE, THEN, IS NOT AN ACT, BUT A HABIT.

—Will Durant

When you
press the
pause button
on a machine,
it stops.

But when you press the pause button on human beings, they start.

—DOV SEIDMAN

When we stop
RESISTING
and fighting
our thoughts
and concerns,
the battle stops.

—TAMARA LEVITT

Mindfulness
isn't difficult.
We just need
to remember
to do it.

—SHARON SALZBERG

Mistakes are the portals of DISCOVERY.

—JAMES JOYCE

If you have
your full
attention in
the moment,
you will see
only LOVE.

—DEEPAK CHOPRA

The feeling that any task is a nuisance will soon disappear if it is done in mindfulness.

—THÍCH NHẤT HẠNH

Life has got
TO BE LIVED—
that's all
there is to it.

—ELEANOR ROOSEVELT

IF YOU THINK
YOU ARE
TOO SMALL
TO MAKE A
DIFFERENCE,

TRY SLEEPING WITH A MOSQUITO.

—DALAI LAMA XIV

You yourself,
as much as
anybody else
in the entire
universe,
deserve your
LOVE
and affection.

—SHARON SALZBERG

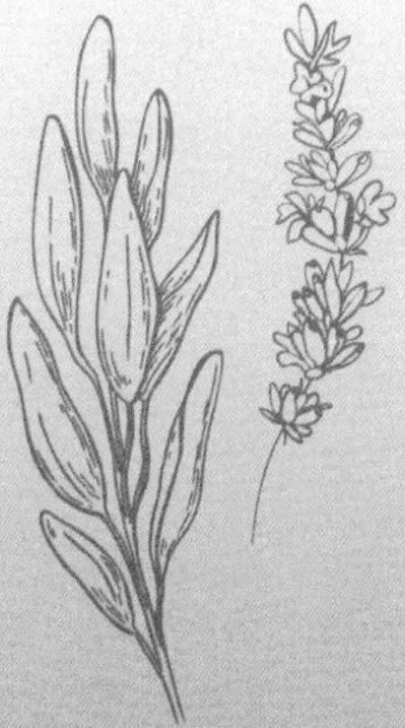

The only person you are destined to become is the person you DECIDE to be.

—RALPH WALDO EMERSON

There are
always flowers
for those
who want to
see them.

—Henri Matisse

Our life
is shaped by
our mind, for
we BECOME
what we think.

—Buddha

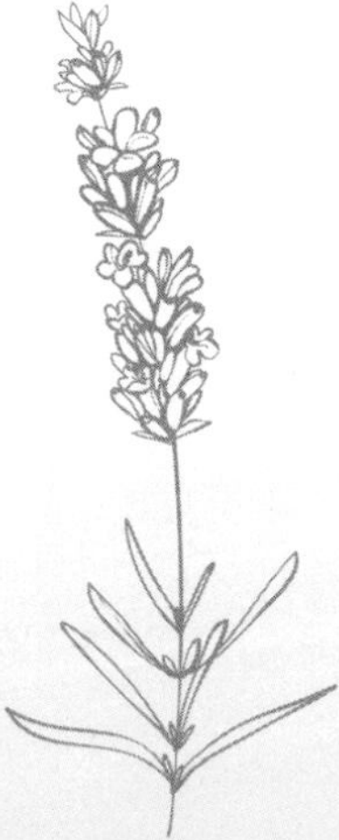

If you want
to conquer
the anxiety of
life, live in the
moment, live
in the breath.

—AMIT RAY

Nowhere can a man find a quieter or more untroubled retreat than in his own SOUL.

—Marcus Aurelius

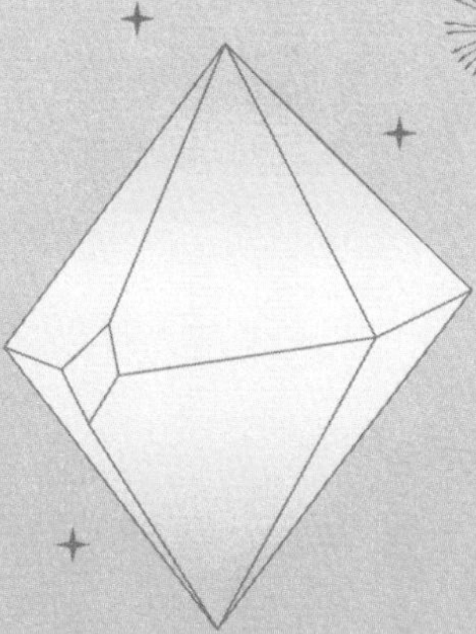

Life is not a
problem to be
solved but a
reality to be
EXPERIENCED.

—SØREN KIERKEGAARD

IT IS
NOT I WHO
CREATE
MYSELF,
RATHER I
HAPPEN TO
MYSELF.

—Carl Jung

TIME IS THE GREATEST INNOVATOR.

—Francis Bacon

Flow with
whatever may
happen, and let
your mind be free.
Stay centered
by accepting
whatever you
are doing. This
is the ultimate.

— CHUANG TZU

FINITE TO FAIL, BUT INFINITE TO VENTURE.

—EMILY DICKINSON

One moment
may with
BLISS repay
Unnumbered
hours of pain.

—THOMAS CAMPBELL

ONE TODAY IS WORTH TWO TOMORROWS.

—Benjamin Franklin

BELIEVE
YOU CAN,
AND YOU'RE
HALFWAY
THERE.

—Theodore Roosevelt

We will develop
and cultivate the
LIBERATION
of mind by
loving kindness,
make it our
vehicle,

make it our
basis, stabilize
it, exercise
ourselves in it,
and fully
PERFECT IT.

—BUDDHA

What lies
behind us and
what lies before
us are but tiny
matters compared
to what lies
WITHIN US.

—HENRY STANLEY
HASKINS

SOMETIMES
THE MOST
IMPORTANT
THING IN THE
WHOLE DAY

IS THE REST
WE TAKE
BETWEEN
TWO BREATHS.

—ETTY HILLESUM

NOTHING
will work unless
YOU DO.

—Maya Angelou

As the
water beads on
a lotus leaf,
as water on
a red lily,
does not adhere,

so the sage
does not adhere
to the seen,
the heard, or
the sensed.

—BUDDHA

The very
center of your
HEART
is where life
BEGINS,
the most
beautiful place
on earth.

—RUMI

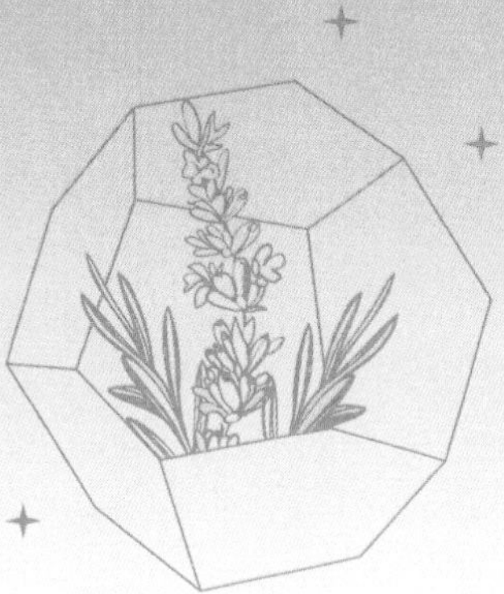

Understanding
is the
heartwood of
well-spoken
words.

—BUDDHA

The truest,
most beautiful
life never
promises to be
an easy one.

We need to
let go of the
lie that it's
supposed to be.

—GLENNON DOYLE

HOW YOU
CLIMB A
MOUNTAIN
IS MORE

IMPORTANT
THAN
REACHING
THE TOP.

—Yvon Chouinard

The only
peace, the only
security, is in
FULFILLMENT.

—HENRY MILLER

Sometimes,
simply by sitting,
the soul collects
WISDOM.

—ZEN PROVERB

PARADISE
is not a place;
it's a state of
consciousness.

—SRI CHINMOY

The teacher
who is indeed
wise does not
bid you to enter
the house of
his wisdom

but rather
leads you to
the threshold
of your mind.

—KAHLIL GIBRAN

Life is like
riding a bicycle.
To keep your
BALANCE,
you must keep
MOVING.

—ALBERT EINSTEIN

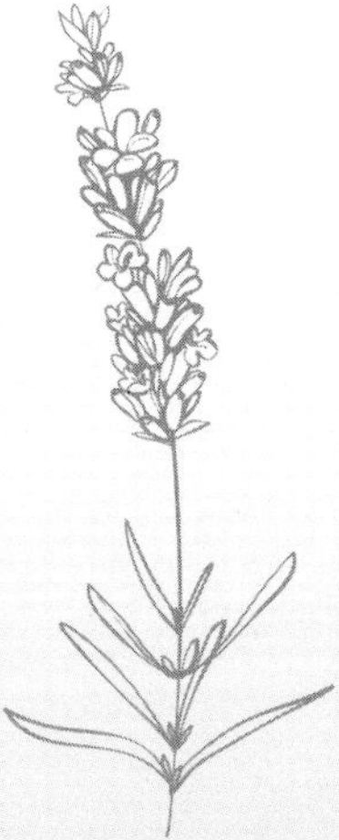

CHERISH
that which is
within you, and
SHUT OFF
that which is
without.

—Chuang Tzu

Altogether,
the idea of
MEDITATION
is not to
create states

of ecstasy or absorption, but to experience BEING.

—CHÖGYAM TRUNGPA

SOMETIMES REJECTION IN LIFE IS REALLY REDIRECTION.

—Tavis Smiley

The subconscious doesn't distinguish sarcasm and jokes. It just accepts what it hears. That's the power of words.

—INDIA ARIE

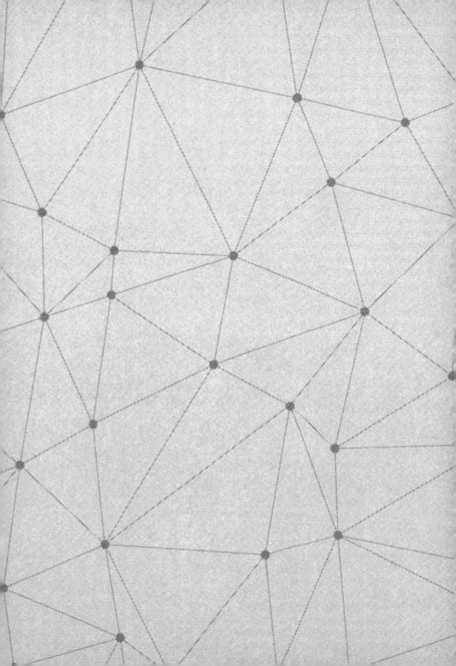

In the midst of
CHAOS,
there is also
OPPORTUNITY.

—SUN TZU

The most
POWERFUL
relationship you
will ever have is
the relationship
with yourself.

—STEVE MARABOLI

First, say to yourself what you would be, and then do what you have to do.

—Epictetus

Forget the past,
and live the
present hour.

—SARAH KNOWLES
BOLTON

TO ME, EVERY
HOUR OF
THE LIGHT
AND DARK IS
A MIRACLE,

EVERY INCH
OF SPACE IS
A MIRACLE.

—Walt Whitman

Don't believe
everything
you think.
Thoughts are
just that—
thoughts.

—ALLAN LOKOS

How you look
at it is pretty
much how
you'll see it.

—RASHEED OGUNLARU

The little
THINGS?
The little
MOMENTS?
They aren't little.

—JON KABAT-ZINN

Happiness is a
butterfly which,
when pursued,
is just beyond
your grasp but,

if you will sit down
quietly, may
alight upon you.

—NATHANIEL
HAWTHORNE

Life is a dance.
Mindfulness is
WATCHING
THE DANCE.

—AMIT RAY

Wherever you are, BE THERE TOTALLY.

—ECKHART TOLLE

TRUTH
is simply
whatever you
can bring
yourself to
BELIEVE.

—ALICE CHILDRESS

Life is really simple, but we insist on making it complicated.

—CONFUCIUS

NOTHING
EVER GOES
AWAY UNTIL IT
HAS TAUGHT
US WHAT
WE NEED
TO KNOW.

—Pema Chödrön

It is only by
EXPRESSING
all that is
INSIDE that
purer and purer
streams come.

—BRENDA UELAND

Any fool can KNOW. The point is to UNDERSTAND.

—ALBERT EINSTEIN

He who knows others is clever, but he who knows himself is enlightened.

—LAO TZU

LIVE ALL
YOU CAN;
IT'S A MISTAKE
NOT TO. IT
DOESN'T
SO MUCH
MATTER

WHAT YOU
DO IN
PARTICULAR,
SO LONG AS
YOU HAVE
YOUR LIFE.

—Henry James

LIFE wastes
itself while
we are
PREPARING
to live.

—Ralph Waldo Emerson

I do not want
the peace
which passeth
understanding;

I want the
understanding
which bringeth
PEACE.

—HELEN KELLER

THESE ARE
THE DAYS
THAT MUST
HAPPEN
TO YOU.

—WALT WHITMAN

It is not what
we do once in
a while that
shapes our lives
but what we do
CONSISTENTLY.

—TONY ROBBINS

CHANGE the
way you look
at things, and
the things you
look at change.

—WAYNE DYER

THE WIND
IS BLOWING.
ADORE THE
WIND!

—PYTHAGORAS

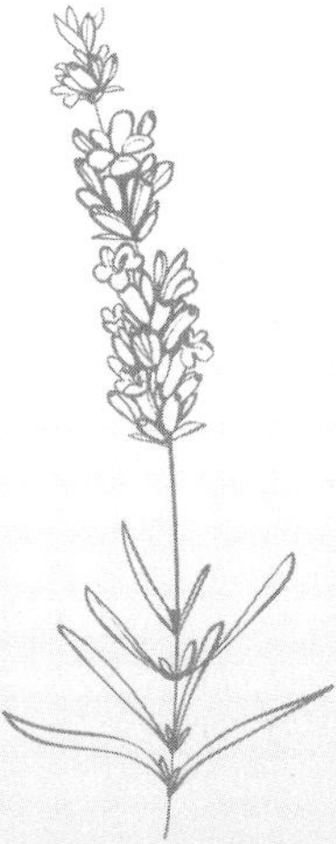

In truth,
to attain to
interior peace,
one must
be willing to
pass through
the contrary
to peace.

—SWAMI BRAHMANANDA

YOU CAN'T STOP THE WAVES, BUT YOU CAN LEARN TO SURF.

—Jon Kabat-Zinn

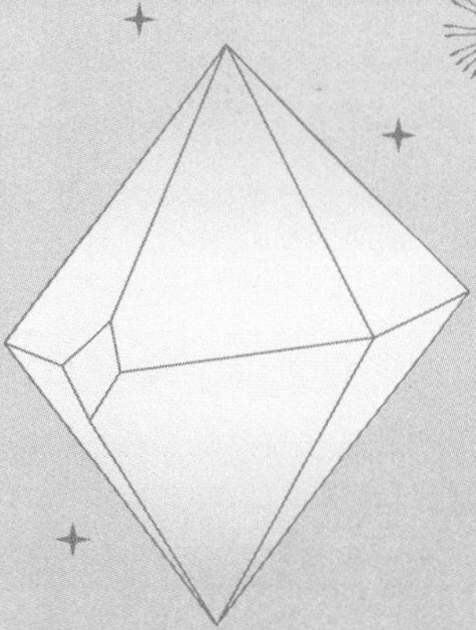

One does
not become
ENLIGHTENED
by imagining
figures of light,
but by making
darkness
CONSCIOUS.

—CARL JUNG

Life can only be understood backwards, but it must be lived FORWARDS.

—SØREN KIERKEGAARD

WHEN I
LET GO OF
WHAT I AM,
I BECOME
WHAT I
MIGHT BE.

—Lao Tzu

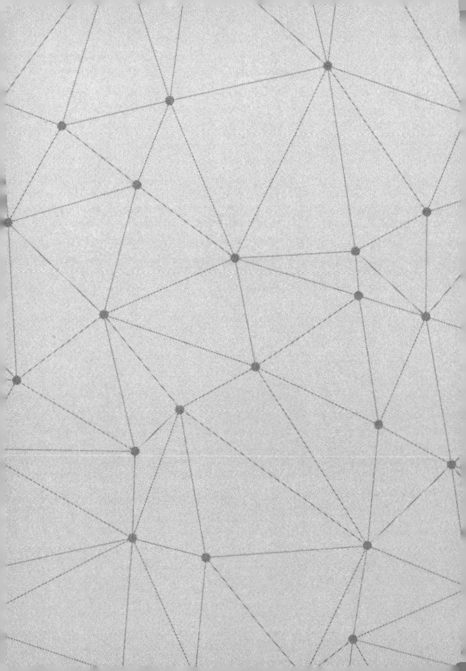

The first rule
is to keep an
untroubled spirit.
The second is
to look things
in the face and
know them for
what they are.

—MARCUS AURELIUS

No great WORK has ever been produced except after a long interval of still and musing MEDITATION.

—WALTER BAGEHOT

To live is so startling it leaves little time for anything else.

—EMILY DICKINSON

There can be no peace without, but through peace within.

—WILLIAM ELLERY CHANNING

BE HAPPY
FOR THIS
MOMENT.
THIS
MOMENT IS
YOUR LIFE.

—Omar Khayyam

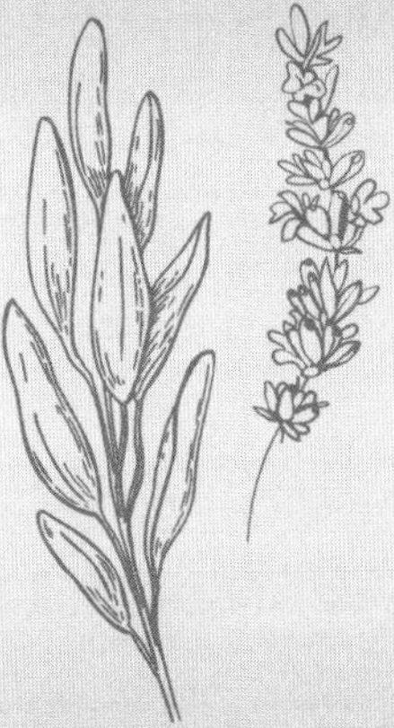

Be patient with yourself. Self-growth is tender; it's holy ground. There's no greater investment.

—STEPHEN COVEY

I have an everyday religion that works for me. Love yourself first, and everything else falls into line.

—LUCILLE BALL

Caring for your body, mind, and spirit is your greatest and grandest responsibility. It's about listening to the needs of your soul and then honoring them.

—KRISTI LING

They told me I didn't understand the assignment, and I told them they didn't understand life.

—JOHN LENNON

When I went to school, they asked me what I wanted to be when I grew up. I wrote down "Happy."

For those of you who
struggle with guilt
regarding self-care,
answer this question:
What greater gift can
you give to those
you love than your
own wholeness?

—SHANNON TANNER

Self-care is never selfish, but it may feel that way when you live a frenzied life.

—ARTHUR P. CIARAMICOLI

Saying no can
be the ultimate
self-care.

—CLAUDIA BLACK

The only person you shouldn't be able to live without is you.

—CHRIS MCGEOWN

Love yourself enough to set boundaries. Your time and energy are precious. You get to choose how you use it.

—ANNA TAYLOR

The fact that someone else loves you doesn't rescue you from the project of loving yourself.

—SAHAJ KOHLI

You can't take care of anyone else unless you first take care of yourself.

—MICHAEL HYATT

People pleasing doesn't allow you to receive.

—ABIOLA ABRAMS

Self-discipline
is self-caring.

—M. SCOTT PECK

You have been criticizing yourself for years, and it hasn't worked. Try approving of yourself and see what happens.

—LOUISE L. HAY

You may be the
only person left who
believes in you, but it's
enough. It takes just
one star to pierce a
universe of darkness.
Never give up.

—RICHELLE E. GOODRICH

They called her witch because she knew how to heal herself.

—TÉ V. SMITH

Most people are about as happy as they make up their minds to be.

—ABRAHAM LINCOLN

Self-care is taking all the pressures you are facing right now, and deciding to which you will respond, and how.

—IMANI SHOLA

When you take care of yourself, you're a better person for others. When you feel good about yourself, you treat others better.

—SOLANGE KNOWLES

If you do not respect your own wishes, no one else will. You will simply attract people who disrespect you as much as you do.

—VIRONIKA TUGALEVA

You've got to learn
to leave the table
when love's no
longer being served.

—NINA SIMONE

Don't be reckless with other people's hearts, don't put up with those who are reckless with yours.

—BAZ LUHRMANN

It's all about falling in love with yourself and sharing that love with someone who appreciates you, rather than looking for love to compensate for a self-love deficit.

—EARTHA KITT

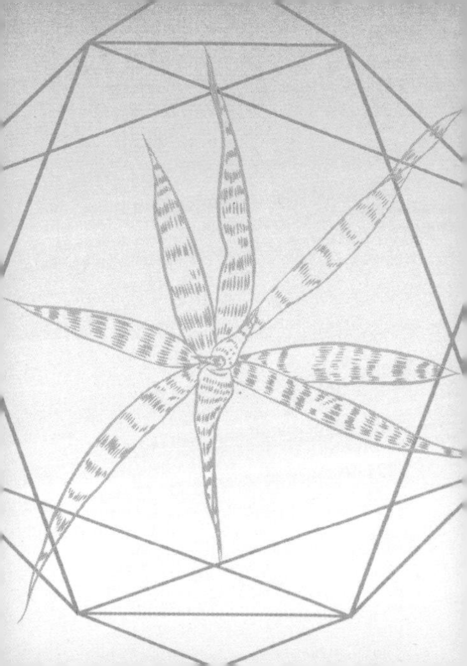

Don't waste your energy trying to change opinions. Do your thing, and don't care if they like it.

—TINA FEY

Your time is way too valuable to be wasting on people that can't accept who you are.

—TURCOIS OMINEK

The love and attention you always thought you wanted from someone else is the love and attention you first need to give to yourself.

—BRYANT MCGILLNS

Do something every day that is loving toward your body and gives you the opportunity to enjoy the sensations of your body.

—GOLDA PORETSKY

Everybody is different, and every body is different.

—BEVERLY DIÉHL

We can't be so
desperate for love
that we forget
where we can
always find it:
within.

—ALEXANDRA ELLE

One does not
get better, but
different and older,
and that is always
a pleasure.

—GERTRUDE STEIN

If we give our children sound self-love, they will be able to deal with whatever life puts before them.

—bell hooks

fresh air, and freedom
to bloom into its
most precious and
beautiful form. This,
my friend, is self-love.

—MIYA YAMANOUCHI

Our soul is like a soft and gentle flower, it needs to be nurtured, cared for, tended to, with sufficient sunlight,

Replace your vicious stress cycle with a vicious cycle of self-care.

—DR. SARA GOTTFRIED

When we self-regulate well, we are better able to control the trajectory of our emotional lives and resulting actions based on our values and sense of purpose.

—AMY LEIGH MERCREE

Though no one can go back and make a brand-new start, anyone can start from now and make a brand-new ending.

—CARL BARD

Take care of your mind, your body will thank you. Take care of your body, your mind will thank you.

—DEBBIE HAMPTON

Setting boundaries
is a way of caring
for myself. It doesn't
make me mean,
selfish, or uncaring
because I don't do
things your way. I care
about me too.

—CHRISTINE MORGAN

When the body forces you to stop, it's saying, "Hey buddy, you've gone too far."

—JACQUELINE ESCOLME

Take care of your body. It's the only place you have to live.

—JIM ROHN

Talk to yourself like you would to someone you love.

—BRENÉ BROWN

Take rest; a field that has rested gives a bountiful crop.

—OVID

After joy, grief;
after grief, joy.

—TAMIL PROVERB

No more
martyring myself.

—SHARON E. RAINEY

We are strong enough to stand tall tearlessly, we are brave enough to bend to cry, and we are sad enough to know that we must laugh again.

—NIKKI GIOVANNI

Letting go is
an inside job,
something only we
can do for ourselves.

—SHARON SALZBERG

The most
terrifying thing is
to accept oneself
completely.

—CARL JUNG

Life shrinks
or expands in
proportion to
one's courage.

—ANAÏS NIN

Observe your comfort level when it comes to being good to yourself. Discomfort is a wise teacher.

—CAROLINE MYSS

When you can't find your purpose in a day, make it to look after yourself.

—DODIE CLARK

Don't ask what the world needs. Ask what makes you come alive and go do it. Because what the world needs are more people who have come alive.

—HOWARD THURMAN

You aren't doing "nothing" when you choose to put your well-being first. In fact, this is the key to having everything.

—BRITTANY BURGUNDER

Don't work so hard that you forget to enjoy your life.

—AKIROQ BROST

No one serves
their friends by
grinding themselves
into dust on the
altar of compassion.

—SEANAN MCGUIRE

Have patience with all things, but first with yourself.

—ST. FRANCIS DE SALES

Self-care is not selfish. You cannot serve from an empty vessel.

—ELEANOR BROWNN

Self-care is giving the world the best of you, instead of what's left of you.

—KATIE REED

When you accept
you have to rescue
yourself, then
you're adulting.

—SHARON PEARSON

Happiness is a choice that requires effort at times.

—AESCHYLUS

When admiring other people's gardens, don't forget to tend to your own flowers.

—SANOBER KHAN

It is not abstinence from pleasures that is best, but mastery over them without being worsted.

—ARISTIPPUS

Nourishing yourself in a way that helps you blossom in the direction you want to go is attainable, and you are worth the effort.

—DEBORAH DAY

Life is a combination of magic and pasta.

—FEDERICO FELLINI

Of all forms of caution, caution in love is perhaps the most fatal to true happiness.

—BERTRAND RUSSELL

So throw off the bowlines. Sail away from the safe harbor. Catch the trade winds in your sails. Explore. Dream. Discover.

—MARK TWAIN

Twenty years from now you will be more disappointed by the things that you didn't do than by the ones you did do.

Your mind will answer most questions if you learn to relax and wait for the answer.

—WILLIAM S. BURROUGHS

The reason people
find it so hard to be
happy is that they
always see the past
better than it was, the
present worse than it
is, and the future less
resolved than it will be.

— MARCEL PAGNOL

Choose with no regret. Do what you love. Live as if this is all there is.

—MARY ANNE RADMACHER

Live with intention. Walk to the edge. Listen hard. Practice wellness. Play with abandon. Laugh.

The most powerful relationship you will ever have is the relationship with yourself.

—STEVE MARABOLI

Self-love
seems so often
unrequited.

—ANTHONY POWELL

I love my
rejection slips. They
show me I tried.

—SYLVIA PLATH

Stop searching for happiness in the same place you lost it. Change is not dismantling the old, it's building the new.

—BRIANNA WIEST

I would
rather be happy
than dignified.

—CHARLOTTE BRONTË

The road to
success is always
under construction.

—LILY TOMLIN

There is only
one corner of
the universe you
can be certain of
improving, and that's
your own self.

—ALDOUS HUXLEY

Be a pineapple:
Stand tall, wear
a crown, and be
sweet on the inside.

—KAT GASKIN

Life is always richer
when we're not
playing who we are,
but being who we are.

—BEN KINGSLEY

The only thing that
will make you happy
is being happy with
who you are, and
not who people
think you are.

—GOLDIE HAWN

Joy and life
exist nowhere
but the present.

—MAXINE HONG
KINGSTON

Let reality be reality. Let things flow naturally forward in whatever way they like.

—LAOZI

Life is a series of natural and spontaneous changes. Don't resist them; that only creates sorrow.

You can't dump
one cup of sugar
into the ocean and
expect to get syrup. If
everybody sweetened
her own cup of water,
then things would
begin to change.

—FLORYNCE KENNEDY

It is hard to fail, but it is worse never to have tried to succeed.

—THEODORE ROOSEVELT

Self-care is how you take your power back.

—LALAH DELIA

Self-care should include the cold shower as well as the scented tub.

—MARY CATHERINE BATESON

I think best in a hot bath, with my head tilted back and my feet up high.

—ELIZABETH JANE HOWARD

Caring for myself is
not self-indulgence,
it is self-preservation,
and that is an act of
political warfare.

—AUDRE LORDE

When you recover or discover something that nourishes your soul and brings joy, care enough about yourself to make room for it in your life.

—JEAN SHINODA BOLEN

Enjoy the
simple things.
Enjoy you.

—BROOKE GRIFFIN

Today do
something for you:
Relax, clear your
mind, take a break,
go for a jog, watch
the sunset.

Everything in
moderation—
including moderation.

—OSCAR WILDE

Take time off . . .

The world will
not fall apart
without you.

—MALEBO SEPHODI

Excess on occasion
is exhilarating. It
prevents moderation
from acquiring the
deadening effect
of a habit.

—W. SOMERSET MAUGHAM

Should a person do good, let him do it again and again. Let him find pleasure therein, for blissful is the accumulation of good.

—THE BUDDHA

The happiest person
is the person who
thinks the most
interesting thoughts,
and we grow happier
as we grow older.

—WILLIAM PHELPS

Human beings make life so interesting.

Do you know, that in a universe so full of wonders, they have managed to invent boredom.

—TERRY PRATCHETT

For every minute you are angry you lose sixty seconds of happiness.

—RALPH WALDO EMERSON

It's good to do uncomfortable things. It's weight training for life.

—ANNE LAMOTT

I must learn to be content with being happier than I deserve.

—JANE AUSTEN

Would you prefer the happiness of scratching a mosquito bite or the happiness of not having a mosquito bite in the first place?

—SOGYAL RINPOCHE

Invent your world.
Surround yourself
with people, color,
sounds, and work
that nourish you.

—SARK

Carve out and claim time to care for yourself and kindle your own fire.

—AMY IPPOLITI

Time you enjoy wasting is not wasted time.

—MARTHE TROLY-CURTIN

Accept who you are. Unless you're a serial killer.

—ELLEN DEGENERES

Not just who you
could become
somewhere down
the line.

—KRIS CARR

Accepting yourself is about respecting yourself. It's about honoring yourself right now, here today, in this moment.

Comparison with myself brings improvement, comparison with others brings discontent.

—BETTY JAMIE CHUNG

Don't compare
your beginnings
to someone
else's middle.

—TIM HILLER

Being a successful person is not necessarily defined by what you have achieved, but by what you have overcome.

—FANNIE FLAGG

Don't compare yourself to others. You have no idea what their journey is all about.

—REGINA BRETT

Too many people spend money they haven't earned to buy things they don't want to impress people they don't like.

—WILL ROGERS

If more of us valued food and cheer and song above hoarded gold, it would be a merrier world.

— J.R.R. TOLKIEN

Too many people overvalue what they are not and undervalue what they are.

—MALCOLM S. FORBES

Sometimes the most important thing in a whole day is the rest we take between two deep breaths.

—ETTY HILLESUM

How simple and
frugal a thing is
happiness: a glass
of wine, a roast
chestnut, a wretched
little brazier, the
sound of the sea.

Nothing else.

—NIKOS KAZANTZAKIS

fall
in love
with your solitude.

—RUPI KAUR

Prepare for
mirth, for mirth
becomes a feast.

—WILLIAM SHAKESPEARE

No pessimist
ever discovered
the secret of the
stars or sailed an
uncharted land
or opened a new
doorway for the
human spirit.

—HELEN KELLER

You see things, and you say, "Why?" But I dream things that never were, and I say, "Why not?"

—GEORGE BERNARD SHAW

There is a blessed madness in the human need to go against the grain of cold and scarcity.

—MARGARET STARKEY

The mind is its
own place, and in
itself can make
a heaven of hell,
a hell of heaven.

—JOHN MILTON

You don't have
to see the whole
staircase, just take
the first step.

—MARTIN LUTHER KING, JR.

This is the real
secret of life—to
be completely
engaged with what
you are doing in
the here and now.

—ALAN WATTS

Don't let people pull you into their storm. Pull them into your peace.

—PEMA CHÖDRÖN

One of the best ways you can fight discrimination is by taking good care of yourself. Your survival is not just important; it's an act of revolution.

—DASHANNE STOKES

Caring for your body,
mind, and spirit is
your greatest and
grandest responsibility.
It's about listening
to the needs of
your soul and then
honoring them.

—KRISTI LING

Nothing is better for self-esteem than survival.

—MARTHA GELLHORN

The secret
to happiness is
freedom . . . and the
secret to freedom
is courage.

—THUCYDIDES

I am my own
experiment.
I am my own
work of art.

—MADONNA

If you cannot be a poet, be the poem.

—DAVID CARRADINE

Your life is already artful—waiting, just waiting, for you to make it art.

—TONI MORRISON

There is no stress in the world, only people thinking stressful thoughts and then acting on them.

—WAYNE DYER

No need to hurry.
No need to
sparkle. No need
to be anybody
but oneself.

—VIRGINIA WOOLF

Pleasure is the object, the duty, and the goal of all rational creatures.

—VOLTAIRE

You never
regret being
kind.

—NICOLE SHEPHERD

I'd far rather
be happy than
right any day.

—DOUGLAS ADAMS

Happiness is not in the mere possession of money; it lies in the joy of achievement, in the thrill of creative effort.

—FRANKLIN D. ROOSEVELT

A bookworm in bed with a new novel and a good reading lamp is as much prepared for pleasure as a pretty girl at a college dance.

—PHYLLIS MCGINLEY

Each day was
a challenge of
enjoyment, and he
would plan it out as
a field general plans a
campaign.

—A.E. HOTCHNER

Instead of trying to make your life perfect, give yourself the freedom to make it an adventure, and go ever upward.

—DREW HOUSTON

Life is to be enjoyed, not simply endured. Pleasure and goodness and joy support the pursuit of survival.

—WILLARD GAYLIN

If you look for perfection, you'll never be content.

—LEO TOLSTOY

Don't get high off praises, and don't get too low on critiques.

—JANELLE MONAE

You are not defined by the number of people who like you.

—SADE ANDRIA ZABALA

I stopped looking for someone to love me. I became that person instead.

—RUDY FRANCISCO

If we can't laugh
at ourselves, and
at one another,
in good spirit and
without malice,
then what fun
can be left?

—GEORGE TAKEI

my own beliefs
and habits—anything
that kept me small.
My judgment called it
disloyal. Now I see it
as self-loving.

—KIM MCMILLEN

When I loved
myself enough,
I began leaving
whatever wasn't
healthy. This meant
people, jobs,

It is a strength
to laugh and to
abandon oneself,
to be light.

—FRIDA KAHLO

Happiness is not
something you
postpone for the future;
it is something you
design for the present.

—JIM ROHN

The foolish man
seeks happiness
in the distance,
the wise grows it
under his feet.

—JAMES OPPENHEIM

Happiness is where we find it, but very rarely where we seek it.

—JOHN PETIT SENN

Give me the luxuries of life and I will willingly do without the necessities.

—FRANK LLOYD WRIGHT

Mankind is safer
when men seek
pleasure than when
they seek the power
and the glory.

—GEOFFREY GOBER

The art of being happy lies in the power of extracting happiness from common things.

—HENRY WARD BEECHER

The mystery of life isn't a problem to solve, but a reality to experience.

—FRANK HERBERT

You're always with yourself, so you might as well enjoy the company.

—DIANE VON FÜRSTENBERG

Taking into account
the public's regrettable
lack of taste, it is
incumbent upon you
not to fit in.

—JANEANE GAROFALO

means to fight the hardest battle which any human being can fight; and never stop fighting.

—e. e. cummings

To be nobody but yourself in a world which is doing its best, night and day, to make you everybody else

Can you remember who you were before the world told you who you should be?

—DANIELLE LAPORTE

To invent your own life's meaning is not easy, but it's still allowed, and I think you'll be happier for the trouble.

—BILL WATTERSON

Learn to value yourself, which means: fight for your happiness.

—AYN RAND

Any happiness you get, you've got to make yourself.

—ALICE WALKER

Don't wait for
other people
to be happy
for you.

We may encounter
many defeats,
but we must not
be defeated.

—MAYA ANGELOU

It is better to
light the candle
than to curse
the darkness.

—WILLIAM L.
WATKINSON

Happiness never decreases by being shared.

—THE SOCIETY FOR THE PROMOTION OF BUDDHISM

Thousands of candles can be lighted from a single candle, and the life of the candle will not be shortened.

Happiness, to be dissolved into something complete and great.

—WILLA CATHER

Do anything, but let it produce joy.

—WALT WHITMAN

If this life is a shipwreck, we must not forget to sing in the lifeboats.

—PETER GAY

We should consider every day lost on which we have not danced at least once.

—FRIEDRICH NIETZSCHE

I believe in
kindness. Also in
mischief. Also in
singing, especially
when singing is
not necessarily
prescribed.

—MARY OLIVER

Too many of us
are not living our
dreams because we
are living our fears.

—LES BROWN

You can't wait
for inspiration.
You have to go
after it with a club.

—JACK LONDON

There are days
I drop words of
comfort on myself
like falling leaves and
remember that it is
enough to be taken
care of by myself.

—BRIAN ANDREAS

The happiness of your life depends upon the quality of your thoughts.

—MARCUS AURELIUS

It's better to look at the sky than live there.

—TRUMAN CAPOTE

We have a bad habit, encouraged by pedants and sophisticates, of considering happiness as something rather stupid.

—URSULA K. LE GUIN

The best way to cheer yourself is to try to cheer someone else up.

—MARK TWAIN

Low self-esteem is like driving through life with your hand-brake on.

—MAXWELL MALTZ

Fall in love with yourself until you finally feel like home.

— JUANSEN DIZON

It's always a good idea to do something relaxing prior to making an important decision in your life.

—PAULO COELHO

And now that
you don't have to
be perfect, you
can be good.

—JOHN STEINBECK

You are imperfect, permanently and inevitably flawed. And you are beautiful.

—AMY BLOOM

Forgive yourself.
The supreme act of
forgiveness is when
you can forgive
yourself for all the
wounds you've created
in your own life.

—MIGUEL ANGEL RUIZ

If your compassion does not include yourself, it is incomplete.

—JACK KORNFIELD

Beyond a wholesome discipline, be gentle with yourself.

—MAX ERHMANN

We are what
our thoughts have
made us; so take care
about what you think.
Words are secondary.
Thoughts live; they
travel far.

—SWAMI VIVEKANADA

The greatest weapon against stress is our ability to choose one thought over another.

—WILLIAM JAMES

Of all the judgments we pass in life, none is more important than the judgment we pass on ourselves.

—NATHANIEL BRANDEN

Choose, every day,
to forgive yourself.
You are human, flawed,
and most of all worthy
of love.

— ALISON MALEE

Take responsibility of your own happiness, never put it in other people's hands.

—ROY T. BENNETT

It's not selfish to
love yourself, take
care of yourself,
and make your
happiness a priority.
It's necessary.

—MANDY HALE

Learning to treat ourselves lovingly may at first feel like a dangerous experiment.

—SHARON SALZBERG

Every act of self-care is a powerful declaration: I am on my side; I am on my side; each day I am more and more on my own side.

—SUSAN WEISS BERRY

Self-care has become a new priority—the revelation that it's perfectly permissible to listen to your body and do what it needs.

—FRANCES RYAN

SELF CARE

Meditations & Inspirations

MANDALA

You must
be completely
awake in the
PRESENT to
enjoy the tea.

—THÍCH NHẤT HẠNH

The ultimate
GIFT of
conscious life
is a sense of the
MYSTERY that
encompasses it.

—LEWIS MUMFORD

THINKING
ABOUT
INTERIOR
PEACE
DESTROYS
INTERIOR
PEACE.

THE PATIENT
WHO
CONSTANTLY
FEELS HIS
PULSE IS NOT
GETTING
ANY BETTER.

—Hubert van Zeller

You cannot
control the
RESULTS,
only your
ACTIONS.

—Allan Lokos

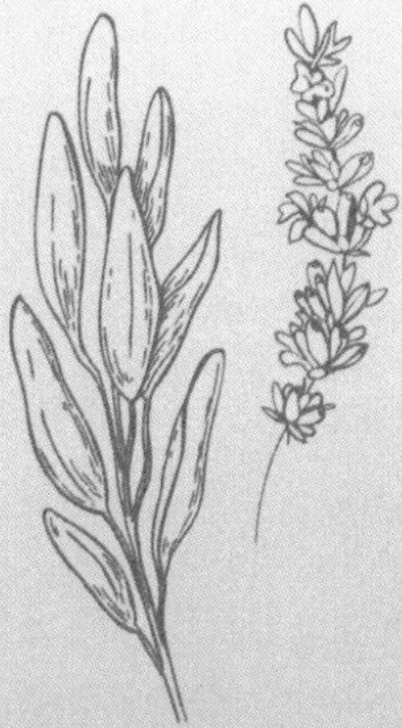

A man who
dares to waste
one hour of
life has not
discovered the
value of life.

—CHARLES DARWIN

If there is to
be any PEACE,
it will come
through being,
not having.

—HENRY MILLER

LIVING
WELL AND
BEAUTIFULLY
AND JUSTLY
ARE ALL ONE
THING.

—Socrates

Every time we
become aware
of a thought,
as opposed to
being lost in
a thought,

we experience
that OPENING
of THE MIND.

—JOSEPH GOLDSTEIN

WAVES
ARE THE
PRACTICE
OF WATER.

—Shunryu Suzuki

Happiness is
when what you
think, what you
say, and what
you do are in
HARMONY.

—MAHATMA GANDHI

Surrender is
a journey from
the outer turmoil
to the
INNER PEACE.

—SRI CHINMOY

Happiness is
your nature. It
is not wrong to
desire it.

What is wrong
is seeking it
outside when
it is inside.

—RAMANA MAHARSHI

There is
something
wonderfully bold
and liberating
about saying
YES to our
entire imperfect
and messy life.

—TARA BRACH

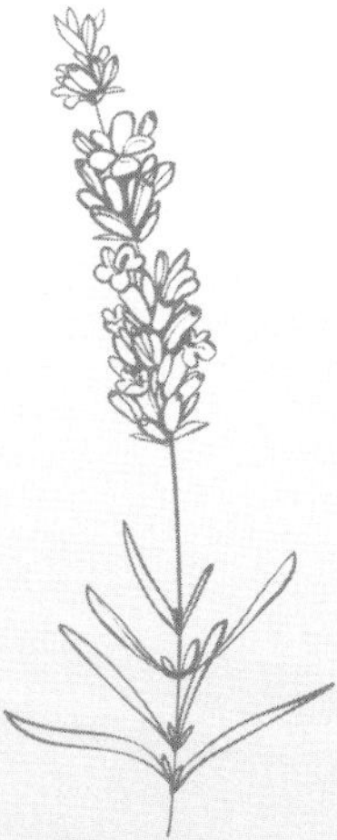

SMILE,
BREATHE,
AND GO
SLOWLY.

—Thích Nhất Hạnh

In this moment, there is plenty of time. In this moment, you are precisely as you should be.

In this moment,
there is INFINITE
POSSIBILITY.

—VICTORIA MORAN

To know what
you know and
what you do not
know, that is
true knowledge.

—CONFUCIUS

WITH THE
NEW DAY
COMES NEW
STRENGTH
AND NEW
THOUGHTS.

—Eleanor Roosevelt

There's only one corner of the universe you can be certain of improving,

and that's your
OWN SELF.

—ALDOUS HUXLEY

IN ANY MOMENT, we can find grounding in the breath.

—TAMARA LEVITT

If you aren't
in the moment,
you are
either looking
FORWARD to
uncertainty or
BACK to pain
and regret.

—JIM CARREY

The SECRET
of contentment
is knowing how
to enjoy what
you have and

PATIENCE is not the ability to wait but how you act while you're waiting.

—JOYCE MEYER

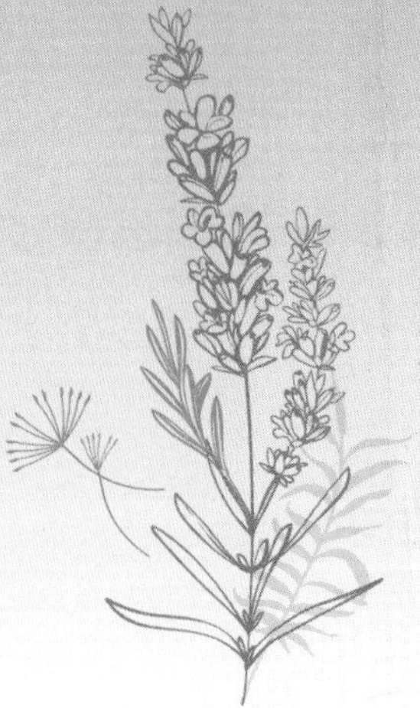

He who
knows all the
ANSWERS
has not been
asked all the
QUESTIONS.

—CONFUCIUS

A journey
of a thousand
miles begins
with a single
STEP.

—LAO TZU

IT IS A
PEACEFUL
THING TO
BE THE ONE
SUCCEEDING.

—Gertrude Stein

Learn silence.
With the quiet
serenity of a
meditative mind,
listen, absorb,
transcribe, and
transform.

—PYTHAGORAS

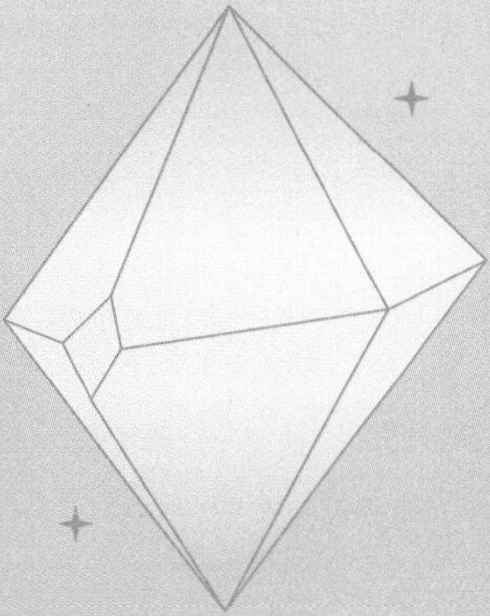

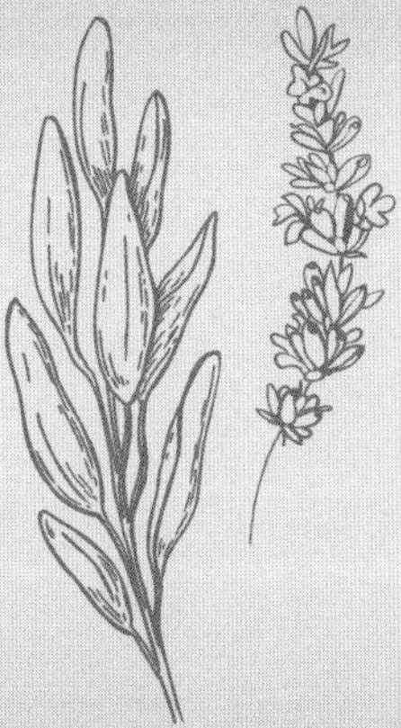

Put your
HEART, MIND,
and SOUL
into even your
smallest acts.
This is the secret
of success.

—SWAMI SIVANANDA

You leave old
habits behind
by starting
out with the
thought,

"I release the need for this in my life."

—WAYNE DYER

YOUR
HEART IS
THE SIZE OF
AN OCEAN.

I DWELL IN POSSIBILITY.

—Emily Dickinson

When you bow,
you should
JUST BOW;
when you sit,
you should JUST
SIT; when you
eat, you should
JUST EAT.

—SHUNRYU SUZUKI

WE FORGET
THE CHAINS
WE WEAR
IN LIFE.

—CHARLES DICKENS

RESOLUTELY
TRAIN
YOURSELF
TO ATTAIN
PEACE.

—Buddha

key to being
alive in a full,
unrestricted, and
inspired way.

—PEMA CHÖDRÖN

Being satisfied
and grateful
with what we
already have is a
magical golden

I AM AN
EXPRESSION
OF THE
DIVINE.

—Alice Walker

can you receive
whatever gift,
lesson, or delight
that moment
has to offer.

—BARBARA DE ANGELIS

Only when your
consciousness
is totally
focused on the
MOMENT
you are in

WE OWN
NO PAST,
NO FUTURE,
WE ONLY
POSSESS
NOW.

—Mary Baker Eddy

YOU ARE
THE SKY.
EVERYTHING
ELSE IS
JUST THE
WEATHER.

—Pema Chödrön

to be able to
lose all desires
for things
BEYOND
YOUR REACH.

—LIN YUTANG